Through My Eyes: Poems of a Prodigy

Prabhjot Bhatia

BookLeaf
Publishing

India | USA | UK

Presentation by *BookLeaf Publishing*

Web: www.bookleafpub.com

E-mail: info@bookleafpub.com

ISBN: 9789363313071

First edition 2024

*This book is dedicated to my beloved mother,
Dalpreet Kaur. Your unwavering love, support,
and belief in me have been the driving forces
behind all my achievements. Thank you for
teaching me the value of hard work, kindness,
and resilience.*

*To my father, Kuldeep Singh Bhatia, for
sparking my initial curiosity and for always
standing by my side.*

*And to every young dreamer out there, may
these poems inspire you to pursue your
passions and embrace the journey with
determination and hope.*

With all my love and gratitude,

Prabhjot Bhatia

ACKNOWLEDGEMENT

I would like to express my deepest gratitude to everyone who has supported me on this incredible journey.

First and foremost, my heartfelt thanks go to my parents, Kuldeep Singh Bhatia and Dalpreet Kaur Bhatia, whose unwavering support and encouragement have been the foundation of my success. Dad, your initial reluctance turned into immense support, and for that, I am forever grateful. Mom, your constant belief in me and your ability to balance everything with grace continue to inspire me every day.

I would also like to thank my Nana and Nani, Sardar Gulshran Singh Digwa and Satnam Kaur, whose love and wisdom have been the sunshine of my life. Their constant presence has been a source of strength and guidance. Nana's life lessons and Nani's nurturing spirit have shaped me into who I am today. You both have always been there for me, and I am forever grateful. Your love has been my greatest blessing.

To my shooting coaches, Gopal Dubey and Vinod Mishra, your guidance, patience, and dedication have been instrumental in honing my skills and achieving my goals. You saw potential in me and helped me realize it through countless hours of practice and encouragement.

I would also like to thank my fellow shooters and friends, whose camaraderie and support have made this journey enjoyable and memorable. Your encouragement and friendly competition have pushed me to be my best.

Finally, this book would not have been possible without the inspiration drawn from my experiences in shooting and the life lessons learned along the way. Each poem is a reflection of my journey, capturing moments of triumph, challenge, and growth. I hope that my words resonate with readers and inspire them to pursue their passions with dedication and creativity.

Thank you all for being a part of my story.
Prabhjot Bhatia

PREFACE

Welcome to *Through My Eyes: Poems of a Prodigy*. I am Prabhjot Bhatia, a 14-year-old poet and shooting enthusiast from Raipur. This collection of poems is a reflection of my journey, thoughts, and experiences as I navigate the world with curiosity and passion.

From the thrill of hitting my first perfect shot in shooting to the profound moments of introspection and empathy, my poems capture the essence of my life. Each verse is a window into my soul, revealing the joys, challenges, and dreams that shape my young existence.

Through My Eyes is not just about my achievements in shooting or my love for poetry. It is about the universal themes that connect us all—education, family, empathy, environmental concerns, and the pursuit of peace. I believe that poetry has the power to touch hearts and provoke thought, and I hope that my words resonate with readers of all ages.

As you turn these pages, you will journey with me through various emotions and experiences. You will see the world as I see it, through the eyes of a prodigy who dreams big and strives for excellence. My hope is that my poems inspire you to reflect on your own life, to appreciate the beauty around you, and to pursue your passions with unwavering dedication.

Thank you for joining me on this poetic adventure. May these poems bring you as much joy and inspiration as they have brought me in writing them.

Warm regards,
Prabhjot Bhatia

Adventures of the Mind

I used to play at Pirates And Sailed the Seven
Seas.
Then I become a cowboy
These simple things did me, please

I had a vivid imagination
Adventure was always on my mind
I discovered the joy of reading
And escaped the daily grind

After all that you lost
Sink deep into the joy for in bedlams made of
chaos,
Everything you want will not be destroyed.

Mom's Inspiration

With every day that passes by,
my respect for my mother skyrockets.
I couldn't be more proud
watching her shine.
She is running a school,
with Papa by her side,
managing it all from the teachers to each of the
students.
It's something that is out of this world,
breaking societal norms.
Coming back home, taking care of her world,
teaches me so many life lessons:
importance of kindness, responsibility,
importance of our religions.
Couldn't be happier to have found a mom in you.

Against Bullying

Encountered something horrific today,
knew the meaning but saw it live today.
For something out of his control,
as if being fat was a crime.
Was called names and defamed;
what a shame.
Wasn't expecting to see it one day
in this so-called woke generation.
And yes, I stood up for him.
Stop them—
fat is not a choice,
certainly not something to make fun of.
Consoled my dear classmate,
it wasn't his fault.
Shall never let someone face this again,
in my class, I will make sure.
Will you?

Environmental Destruction

In forests deep and oceans wide,
is where all the beauty resides.
Is being chopped and populated
by intelligent species: humans—
something that is running our lives,
providing oxygen, water to drink.
Depleting the ozone layer,
increasing the temperature,
plastic thrown everywhere I lay my eyes,
clogging the world.
Forest fires,
earthquakes and floods—
heard of man-made disasters.
Intelligent beings are such poison,
causing damage to the earth,
plant that has nourished us.
Each step we take is to save,
will extinct us.
Will we be able to save the earth?

Call for Empathy

In words unkind and actions rash,
I see pain in every lash.
Been told it's not the lasher's fault—
a feeble-minded soul
can't see the world through clear glass.
Let me lend you a cloth,
wipe the dirt off.
If you can't speak soft,
don't speak at all.
Let's open our hearts and minds,
accept every kind,
create a world where empathy expands,
where we can walk hand in hand.

Peace

6

Can't seem to understand
something so basic:
maintaining world peace
is a task unfathomable to some souls.
People dying in gun violence,
small children dying in school—
but for what?
To rule over each other,
to command or control someone?
I have never felt the need
to control.
What must be lacking
to take such measures?
Don't you light up when people smile?
Isn't peace something that comes to your mind?
Will I be harmed soon?

Lesson of Discipline

Was irritating to me,
what's this discipline?
Papa keeping me in check,
get up before dawn,
keep myself clean,
pray to God,
focus on my studies—
why the badgering?
Why must it be done every day?
Didn't understand the significance.
Discipline is what made the successful today.
I am a successful shooter
with practice and discipline.
I can't thank Papa
enough for this valuable lesson
that he taught me each day.

Family Harmony

In family dinners and bedtime tales,
I find comfort in family trails—
a loving family of four:
my mother, father, brother, and I.
Harmony here that resides,
my home is where
all the worry subsides.
My mother teaches me kindness, love,
father teaches me discipline,
my brother teaches tolerance
because I need the energy to tolerate
my oh-so-crazy brother.
So yes, I am blessed
to have found a family in you all.
Love you.

Sportsmanship and Pride

With sweat and tears,
I strive to win.
Sportsmanship lessons
found within,
I give my all,
come what may,
will never lose aim
to hit the perfect game.
That's my claim,
won many gold medals
to show for.
Not speaking in vain,
this year will be mine—,
the year of our country's fame.
Will win for my country's name,
a proud Indian is what I am,
the least to say.
Jai Hind.

Mother Earth's Call

Beneath the sky so vast and blue,
I see Earth in need of rescue.
With every tree that is cut in vain,
Mother Nature cries in pain.
Every plastic we throw,
Mother chokes in pain.
Every building we build,
Mother Nature cries a flood.
Every flood it causes,
destroys everything we build,
destroys our chances
to save water.
Why is this hard to understand?
You, my reader,
promise me to love our mother,
Mother Nature, Mother Earth.

Parents' Strength

I can't help but notice
how strong my parents are,
working hard and making our home.
One runs a school,
the other handles it all,
yet still show up for me,
always there for me,
teaching me all-important life lessons,
educating the importance of my religion.
I am growing to make them proud,
I hope I do.

Bond of Friendship

In laughter shared and in secrets kept,
a bond of steel yet as light as air.
Through some days of joy,
some nights of tears,
we stand as one,
a duo rare.
I am lucky to be in this pair,
sure we fight sometimes,
but we can't stay apart.
We have so much fun,
sometimes mistaken as brothers—
to say the least, couldn't imagine a better friend,
my best friend.

Self-Reflection

In the mirror's gaze,
I seek to find
the depth of me within my mind.
A puzzle piece
to understand the self I hold—
what are my limits?
How high can I fly?
Will my wings be able
to carry the weight
of the dreams I retain
to the heights I want to obtain?
Even if it is forbidden,
in caves in undiscovered jungles,
I want it all.
If I could,
I would ask mirror, mirror on the wall,
will I be able to achieve it all?

Gratitude and Relief

Mask worn,
in hands we wash,
yet the virus still hit us hard.
My father was entangled
with the sickly virus,
the COVID-19.
Scared the living bone out of everybody,
Papa is our backbone.
God forbid something
happened to that pure soul,
but after a week of despair,
Papa came back,
all nursed back to health.
Thank God for curing my father.

New School Year

A new school year, a fresh start,
Nervous feelings in my heart.
New faces, new acquaintances to make,
New challenges I must take.
The hallways bustle with energetic chatter,
Excitement blended with a little disarray.
Books and backpacks, lockers and keys,
Teachers calling out names with ease.
I'll study hard and do my best,
Give it my all and pass each test.
With every lesson, I'll develop and learn,
And for fresh experiences, I'll always yearn.
Math and physics, history too,
Art and music, something fresh.
Each subject a door to a different place,
Expanding my thinking, setting the tempo.
Here's to a year of progress and cheer,
A time to thrive, a time to steer.
With hope and dreams, I'll persevere,
In this path, I'll vanquish every fear.

Starry Night

Lying in the grass at night,
The sky above is such a sight.
Stars glitter like a million dreams,
Casting down their gleaming light.
The moon shines softly, a guiding light,
Illuminating the serene night.
In this wide expanse, I feel so small,
Yet connected to it all.
I wish upon a shooting star,
Wondering whether it flies far.
Will my wish come true one day?
Under this starry sky, I pray.
The constellations tell stories old,
Of heroes, lovers, and fortunes bold.
I trace their paths with interested eyes,
In the quiet, under the boundless skies.

My Little Sister

She's small and often a pest,
But my little sister is the best.
Her giggles fill the house with cheer,
Even while she's pulling my ear.
We play pretend and make up stories,
Share secrets and our tiny worries.
She looks up to me, and that's a fact,
I'm her protector, I've got her back.
Her small hands in mine feel right,
Together we face each day and night.
Her smile is a beacon, her laughter a song,
In her company, I feel strong.

The Big Game

Nervous butterflies in my chest,
It's time to do my very best.
The crowd is cheering, the stakes are high,
But I'll do my best, I won't be shy.
Every pass, every shot,
I'm giving it all I've got.
The whistle blows, the game begins,
With determination, my team will win.
Sweat streams down, my muscles ache,
But there's no time for a single break.
Focus intense, heart pumping fast,
Every moment, make it last.

Summer Vacation

Summer days so long and bright,
Filled with laughter from dawn to night.
The sun, our constant companion in the sky,
Chasing clouds away, making us feel high.
Ice cream, swimming, and bike trips too,
Freedom to do what we want to do.
No schoolwork or school alarms,
Just endless days on Grandpa's yard.
Waking up to birds' beautiful melody,
Playing outside all day long.
Picking berries, climbing trees,
These are the times that make me feel free.

A Friend's Goodbye

The time has come to say farewell,
To a friend who knows me all too well.
Through laughter and tears, joy and pain,
In sunshine and in pouring rain.
We've walked this path side by side,
With trust and love as our guide.
But now, my friend, you must depart,
Leaving a void in my heart.
Memories we made, moments we shared,
In those times, we truly cared.
Though distance may keep us apart,
You'll always have a place in my heart.

Dreams of Tomorrow

As I lie beneath the starry night,
My mind takes flight in dreams so bright.
Visions of tomorrow fill my head,
Of all the paths that lie ahead.
I dream of places far and wide,
Of adventures that can't be denied.
Climbing mountains, crossing seas,
In a world where I am free.
I see myself in future days,
Finding strength in different ways.
Overcoming fears, embracing change,
In a life that's full and strange.

Proud

22

In order of this world
I want to be distortion
In the stream of the river
I want to be an obstruction
I want to stand out
Like a flag on the pole.
I want to make my family proud.

Goals

Shoot the goals as I aim
Miss the ones that might
help me later gain
Now I understand,
Not every opportunity
is a must-grab
Some might strike and gain
And rest I learn a lesson
To play better again.

Unfolding

Like the petals of a flower
I slowly bloom,
In a garden of confusion,
I find my room.
I stretch towards the light, unsure and afraid,
But,
Knowing that in growth,
I've truly made.
Each thorn I carry,
A mark of pain,
But through it all,
I'll bloom again.
The seasons shift, and I evolve,
What once was doubt,
now I resolve.
I am not perfect,
I am not whole,
But every piece makes up my soul.

Becoming

I am not what I was yesterday,
And tomorrow,
I'll change again.
A butterfly trapped inside a shell,
Breaking free with each step I dwell.
The world will tell me who to be,
But I'll carve my own identity.
With every tear and every smile,
I'm learning who I am, all the while.
I stumble, I fall, I learn, I rise,
I'm growing beneath a changing sky.

The Road Within

The journey I walk is mine alone,
Through forests dense,
through lands unknown.
I search for answers,
for who I'll be,
In the shadows of my uncertainty.
But every road leads back to me,
In every flaw, in every plea.
I am not a story yet complete,
But on each page,
I find my feet.
No one can tell me how to grow,
For only I will truly know.

The Mountain's Call

The mountain calls,
its voice so deep,
A promise in each rocky sweep.
I climb, unsure, yet full of grace,
In its heights, I find my place.
Each step I take is hard and slow,
But in the struggle,
my spirit grows.
For nature shows me I am strong,
That even in the climb, I belong.
The mountain and I,
we rise as one,
Until the journey is fully done.

Letting Go

I hold the grudge like a thorny vine,
Wrapped around this heart of mine.
But in its grip,
I lose my way,
Carried deeper into the gray.
Yet when I loosen and release,
I find my heart can finally breathe.
Forgiveness isn't weakness, no,
It's strength that lets the spirit grow.
So I let go, not for their sake,
But for the peace that's mine to take.

Social Media

All I see is hands and no faces
Embedded in the sin of the era
Our mobile phones
Every friend would rather PUBG
Then play on the ground.
My parents too have included
The poison over the dining tables
They work, I get it.
But I do not understand
Why can't people just look up?

Forgiveness

I can't comprehend
being lied to.
I was specific with my friends
Isn't something I would tolerate.
I have made mistakes.
So many that I've lost count.
Mom explained that if I forgive myself
Must not repeat it again.
So I shall give my friends a chance
To persevere.

Let Go

I began with "never could,"
But now I'm learning.
To let go of anger
Piled up in my gut.
I remember my mother's face—
Her teachings; and it passes away.

Roots and Rain

32

The earth beneath my feet is old,
A story in every grain of gold.
I feel the rain, soft and slow,
Washing away the weight I know.
Like roots that dig so deep below,
I too am grounded in what I sow.

Through My Eyes

The world feels big, too big for me,
At fourteen, I'm still trying to see
Where I belong, what's right, what's true,
In a maze of faces, skies so blue.

I'm caught between a child and man,
Holding dreams I barely understand.
A racing heart, a restless mind,
Searching for answers I may not find.

School hallways echo with whispered words,
Some are sharp, some never heard.
I laugh, I stumble, I try to fit,
But alone in my room, none of it clicks.

A Rainy Day

34

The raindrops dance on my windowpane,
Washing away my silent pain.
Sitting in the classroom.
Watching the droplet drain.
The petals of the flower vase.

Identity

I'm searching for who I'm meant to be,
In a world that tries to define me.
For I haven't asked for the world's help.
I already have predefined my destiny.
Shooting for the stars is my journey.

Memories

36

Faded pictures, echoes of the past,
Moments fleeting, yet they seem to last.
My childhood exists just in my photographs.
In memories, I remember it all.
Playing with my brother
Laughing it off.
Fighting till we tear each other's neck off.
All of it, I remember it all.

Growing Up

The world seems big, so vast, so wide,
But I will learn to walk with pride.
Through ups and downs, I'll find my way,
And grow a little every day.
With every step, I'll rise and stand,
For life is placed within my hand.

A Secret Place

38

I have a place, it's all my own,
Where I can go and be alone.
A secret spot, no one can see,
A world that's made for only me.
In this place, my mind can rest,
And I can be my very best.

Endings and Beginnings

With every end, a new beginning grows,
A different path, a world that shows.
Though endings bring a touch of pain,
Beginnings bring the chance again.
So when the curtain starts to fall,
Remember, there's more to it all.

A World of Color

40

The world is painted bold and bright,
A canvas full of pure delight.
Each color tells a different tale,
From golden suns to blue-hued sails.
In every shade, a story blooms,
A world of color in every room.

The Fear of Change

Change is scary, change is new,
It makes you wonder what to do.
But in the fear, there's courage too,
A chance to start, a chance to view.
So even though the road ahead looks strange,
Take a step and embrace the change.

Seasons

42

Spring's flowers bloom, a fresh new start,
Summer's warmth fills every heart.
Autumn leaves begin to fall,
Winter's chill then wraps it all.
Each season brings its own delight,
From morning sun to cold moonlight.
The world turns slowly, day by day,
As seasons come and fade away.

The Quiet

The woods are quiet, calm, and deep,
Where ancient trees their secrets keep.
A path that winds through mossy ground,
Where nature's peace is all around.
The birds sing softly in the trees,
A gentle hum upon the breeze.
In this place, my heart finds rest,
Where nature's silence feels the best.

Hope

44

Hope is a light that never dies,
A steady flame beneath the skies.
It guides us through the darkest night,
And shows us that everything's alright.
In every heart, hope finds its way,
And leads us to a brighter day.

Journey

The road was long, the path unknown,
A journey taken all alone.
But with each step, new sights arose,
A mystery only travel knows.
Through mountains high and valleys deep,
Through forests where the shadows creep.
An unexpected path was found,
A journey leading all around.

Courage

Courage is not the absence of fear,
It's taking a step when danger's near.
It's standing tall when others fall,
And answering whenever duty calls.
In every heart, courage resides,
A strength we carry deep inside.

Laughter

Laughter echoes in the air,
A joy that's spread beyond compare.
It starts with one, then grows and grows,
A happiness that overflows.
In every laugh, a spark of light,
A fire that burns away the night.
The world grows brighter with each sound,
As laughter spreads its warmth around.

Kindness in Strangers

48

A smile exchanged with someone new,
A simple act that follows through.
A helping hand, a warm embrace,
A kindness shared in every place.
The world is brighter when we care,
For love and kindness, we can share.
In strangers, we may find a friend,
And spread a kindness that won't end.

Empathy

To walk a mile in someone's shoes,
To feel the weight of others' blues.
In every heart, a story told,
Of struggles hidden, dark and cold.
Empathy's light breaks through the wall,
It lifts us up, it helps us all.
A bridge that spans both near and far,
Connecting souls for who they are.

Unity

50

Together we can rise so high,
Like birds who take to the open sky.
In unity, there's strength we find,
A power that can change mankind.
When hands are joined and hearts aligned,
A better world is redefined.
Together, we can fight and win,
For change starts when we all begin.

Equality

Equality is just a dream,
A goal so far, yet close it seems.
We march, we speak, we raise our hand,
For equal rights across the land.
No gender, race, or class should be,
A barrier to being free.
For in the end, we're all the same—
Each human heart, each precious name.

Mental Health

The mind can break, the soul can bend,
A battle fought without an end.
But mental health is real, it's clear,
A struggle many hold so near.
In silence, they may hide their pain,
But with support, there's much to gain.
So let's speak out, let's lift the veil,
For mental health shall not prevail.

Peer Pressure

They push and pull, they try to sway,
To make you act a certain way.
But deep inside, you know what's true,
The choice to make is up to you.
Peer pressure's voice is loud and strong,
But doing right is never wrong.
So stand your ground, don't fall or sway,
For you control your own pathway.

Responsibility

54

The earth is crying, loud and clear,
Its voice is filled with pain and fear.
We take and take without a care,
Forgetting that it's ours to share.
But if we act, if we unite,
We can protect with all our might.
The earth is ours, both you and me,
To guard, preserve, and keep it free.

Immigration

They come from far, from lands unknown,
Seeking a place to call their own.
With hopes and dreams of better days,
They walk a path in foreign ways.
But in their hearts, they're just like you,
With love and pain, with dreams so true.
For every stranger, every friend,
Deserves a place where love won't end.

The Oppressed

56

Their voices stilled, their power lost,
Their lives are caught in fear's great cost.
But in their silence, strength is found,
A quiet roar, a rising sound.
For when the oppressed unite in one,
The battle for freedom has begun.
No chain, no lock can hold them down,
Their time will come to wear the crown.

Divide

In cities bright with screens and light,
Technology is at its height.
But in the corners of the earth,
Some never know the digital birth.
The gap grows wide, it pulls apart,
A difference made right from the start.
But knowledge should be free to share,
For all deserve their rightful share.

Cyberbullying

58

Behind the screen, they throw their words,
A faceless fight that goes unheard.
The damage done, the pain is real,
Though hidden, it's a wound you feel.
But kindness too can spread online,
A digital force, strong and kind.
For every click that shares the hate,
Can be a step to help change the fate.

Child Labor

Small hands that work from dawn till night,
Their childhood lost, out of sight.
For pennies paid, they toil away,
While others live, while others play.
But every child deserves to dream,
To chase the stars, to laugh, to scream.
So let's protect the young and free,
And give them back their right to be.

Racism

They judge us by the shades we wear,
But underneath, we're all aware.
Our blood runs red, our hearts all beat,
We're humans born with love complete.
Racism blinds and builds a wall,
But unity will break it all.
For in our hearts, we're all the same,
Each life is worthy of its name.

Hunger

In every corner of the earth,
Some struggle just to find their worth.
With empty plates and hollow eyes,
They wait for help beneath the skies.
But we can fight, we can unite,
To give the hungry back their light.
For no one should be left behind,
In a world with food for all mankind.

Fame

62

They rise to heights so few can see,
But with the light comes scrutiny.
For fame can lift, but also break,
A heavy burden some can't take.
The world will watch, but rarely know,
The pain that often doesn't show.
Behind the fame, behind the name,
There's just a person, all the same.

Blame Game

In aim I strike, it is not always confidence
But fear, anxiety, and focus.
I am criticized for my work
And cheered on my aims on point.
Now,
I understand isn't about me
When I play, I am the game
So blame game,
Doesn't work on me anymore.

Plastic Oceans

64

Bottles, bags, they float and sway,
Turning oceans into dismay.
Turtles trapped, fish can't breathe,
In plastic webs, they cannot leave.
It's time to change the way we live,
Before the sea has no more to give.

A Voice in the Crowd

You say I'm too young to shout,
But I'm here, and I have no doubt.
Marches, protests, signs held high,
Hoping change will paint the sky.
I might be one, but I'm not small,
Together we can stand tall.

The Earth's Plea

The trees are calling, "Let us stand!"
Mountains crumble, seas expand.
We burn the green, we dig the ground,
But nature's screams make no sound.
Don't wait for tomorrow, act today—
The Earth won't heal if we walk away.

Equality's Dream

Equal pay, equal rights,
But why do we still fight these fights?
Skin, gender, faith, or love,
Shouldn't we all rise above?
The dream of equality still feels far,
But I'll keep reaching, star by star.

A World Without Hunger

Empty bowls, silent cries,
Across the world, a child dies.
While some feast, others starve,
Is this how the world should carve?
Food for all, it's not too late—
We can choose to change their fate.

Digital Shadows

Behind the screens, we type and hide,
But words can cut deeper than a knife.
An insult here, a joke too cruel,
But why is kindness the rarest rule?
In this digital world, where hate can thrive,
Can we let compassion be the drive?

Climate's Cry

The ice caps melt, the forests burn,
Yet when will the lesson be learned?
The air we breathe is thick with smoke,
The Earth is drowning, it starts to choke.
If we ignore this loud alarm,
We risk our home, our world, great harm.

Education for All

They dream of books they'll never see,
Locked from the future's key.
While some of us learn and grow,
Others will never know.
Let's break the chains and build a bridge,
Let knowledge flow across every ridge.